This book is a special gift for

_____

From: _____

To my brother Larry,
the best fisherman I know.

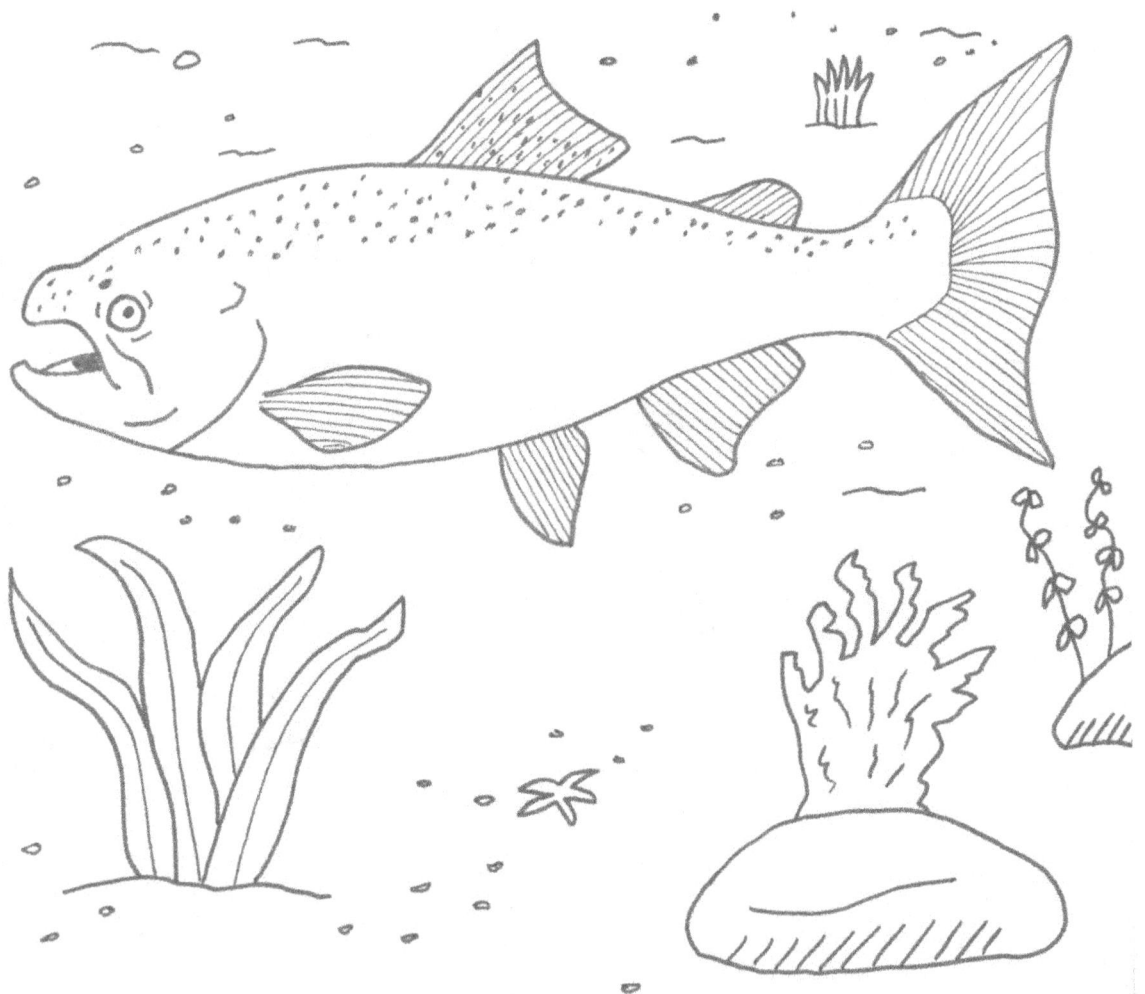

A World of Fish

A Coloring With Dr. C. Trivia Book

Jerry Cavanaugh

A World of Fish: A Coloring Book With Dr. C. Trivia Book
By Jerry Cavanaugh
Cover and Layout by Daniel Traynor

AimHi Press
Orlando, Florida
AimHiPress.com
©2022, Jerry Cavanaugh

Names: Cavanaugh, Jerry. | Traynor, Daniel, Cover, and Layout.
Title: A World of Fish Coloring Book / by Jerry Cavanaugh
Description: Orlando, FL | AimHi Press, 2022. | Summary: Learn about fish with these fun-to-complete coloring pages.
Identifiers: ISBN 978-1-945493-50-8 (paperback)

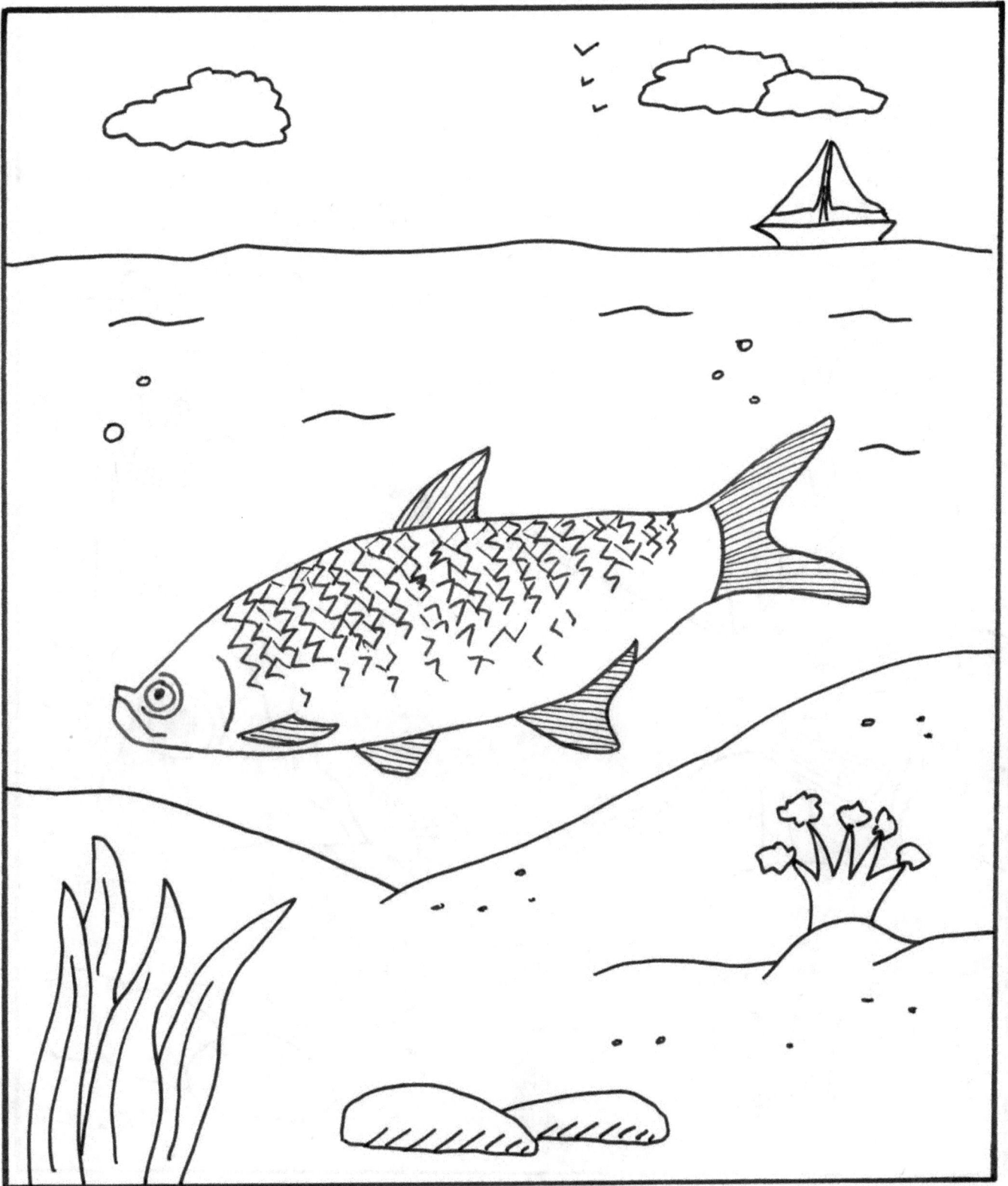

Atlantic Tarpon

(MAGALOPS ATLANTICUS)

The Atlantic Tarpon, also known as the Silver King, is found in the warm parts of the Atlantic Ocean, on the Pacific side of Central America, and sometimes in rivers. It can often grow to 6 feet in length and is a favorite game fish.

Bicolor Parrotfish
(CETOSCARUS BICOLOR)

The Bicolor Parrotfish inhabits the Red Sea and the Indo-Pacific region. It uses its beak-like teeth to scrape the algae off dead coral skeletons. It is a protogynous hermaphrodite, which means that it begins life as a female but gradually transitions to a male. It can grow to 3 feet in length.

Bluehead Wrasse
(THALASSOMA BIFASCIATUM)

The Bluehead Wrasse is a small, energetic fish, reaching only 6 inches in length. It is found in the coral reefs of the Caribbean Sea, near Bermuda and Florida, and in the Gulf of Mexico. It has a lifespan of only two years. It can change color based on its surroundings.

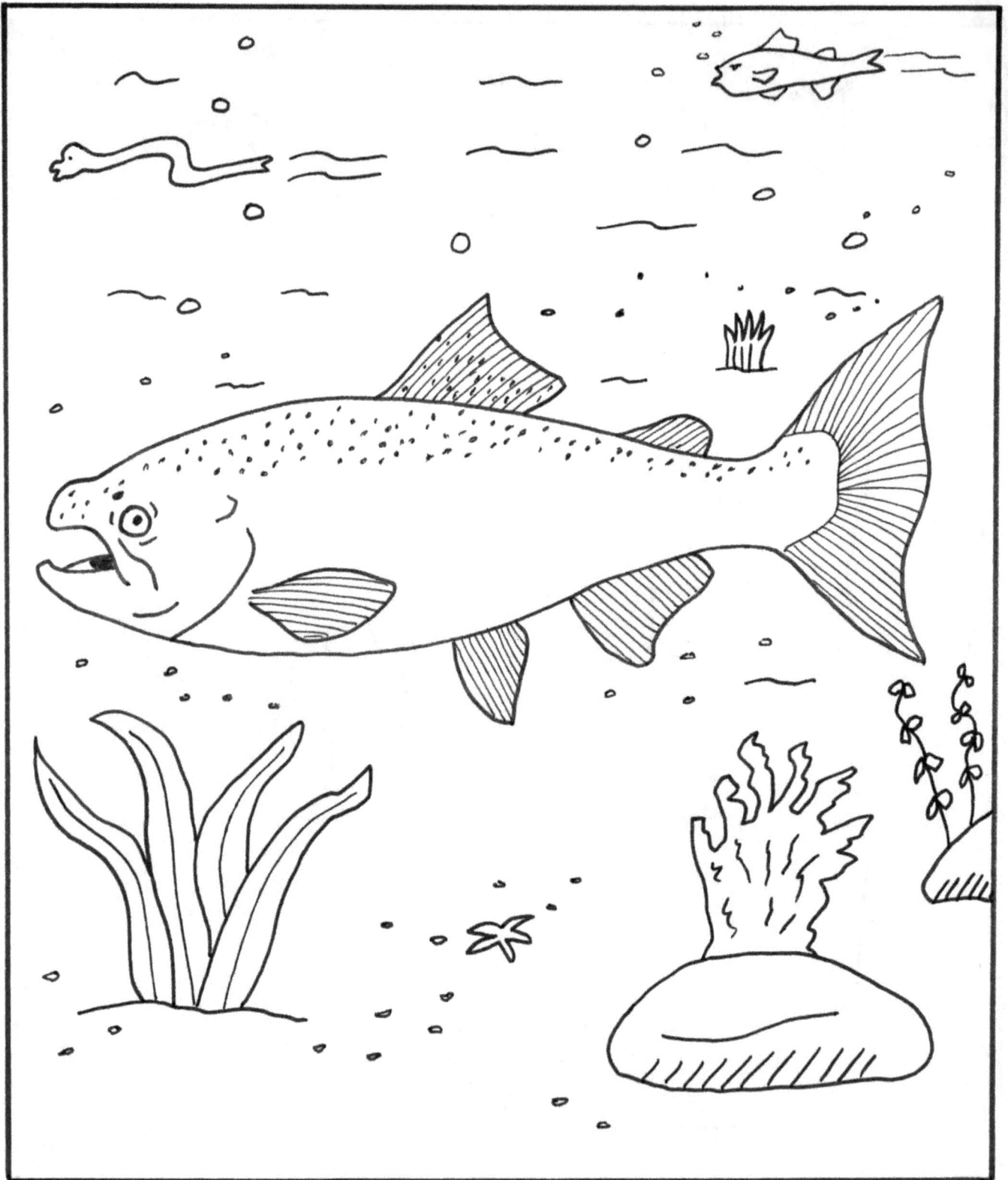

Chinook Salmon
(ONCORHYNCHUS TSHAWYTSCHA)

The Chinook Salmon is the largest of the Pacific salmon in North American waters, with an average length of 3 feet and weight of 30 pounds. It ranges from Alaska to northern California in the eastern Pacific and in the waters off Russia and Japan in the west. The female Chinook salmon may lay from 3,000 to 14,000 eggs in a single nest.

Copperband Butterflyfish

(CHELMON ROSTRATUS)

The Copperband Butterflyfish is one of some 115 or more species of butterflyfish. It is a small fish, reaching from 5.1 to 8 inches in length. It inhabits shallow inshore waters in the coral reefs of the Atlantic, Pacific, and Indian Oceans, and feeds on crustaceans and coral polyps.

Planehead Filefish

(STEPHANOLEPIS HISPIDUS)

The Planehead Filefish lives in seagrass beds and on sand and mud bottoms. It is found in the western Atlantic from Nova Scotia to Brazil and in the eastern Atlantic from Morocco to Angola. It reaches a length of only seven inches at adulthood.

Mahi Mahi

(CORYPHAENA HIPPURUS)

The Mahi Mahi, or Common Dolphinfish, is found throughout the world near the surface of tropical, subtropical, and temperate seas. It is a piscivore, meaning that it preys on fish, squid, and shrimp. It typically reaches 3 feet in length, but can grow as large as 6 feet.

Northern Red Snapper

(LUTJANUS CAMPECHANUS)

The Northern Red Snapper inhabits rocky bottoms, ledges, and artificial reefs, such as offshore oil rigs and shipwrecks, in the western Atlantic, Carribean Sea, and Gulf of Mexico. The average adult is 24 inches long and can weigh up to 50 pounds.

Oceanic Whitetip Shark
(CARCHARHINUS LONGIMANUS)

The Oceanic Whitetip Shark, also known as Brown Milbert's Sand Bar Shark, is a solitary, slow-moving predator that will eat just about anything found in tropical and temperate seas. It averages 9.8 feet in length and weighs up to 370 pounds.

Powder Blue Surgeonfish

(ACANTHURUS LEUCOSTERNON)

The Powder Blue Surgeonfish, also known as the Powder Blue Tang, is found in the Indian Ocean, from South Africa to Indonesia. It has a retractable razor-sharp spine on either side of the base of its tail to keep predators away. In the animated children's film, *Finding Nemo*, one of the central characters was a Powder Blue Surgeonfish named Dory.

Blonde Naso Tang
(NASO ELEGANS)

The Blonde Naso Tang, also know as the Elegant Unicornfish, is found among the corals, seaward reefs, and rocks in lagoons in the Indian Ocean and Red Sea. It can grow to 18 inches in length and live from 30 to 45 years.

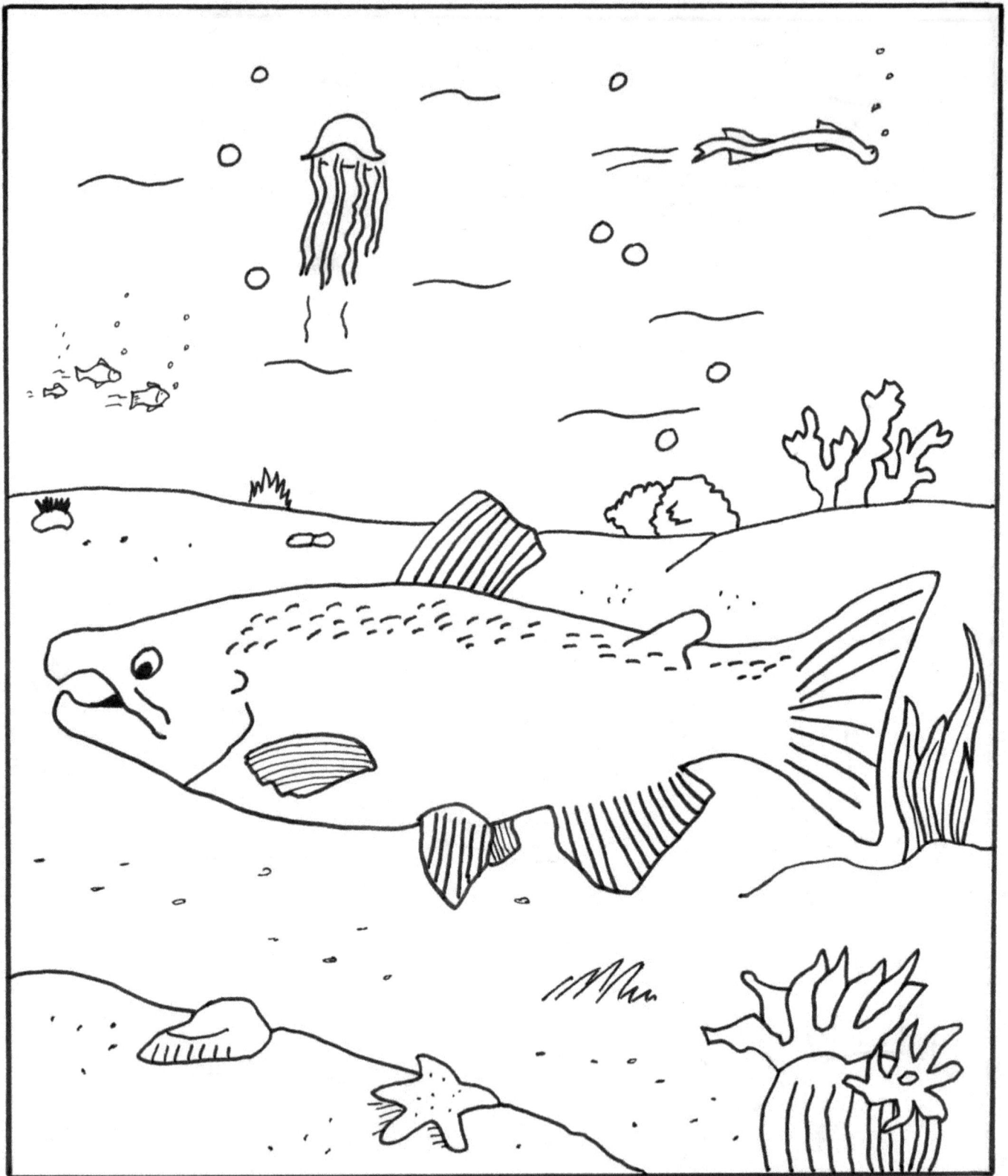

Coho Salmon
(ONCORHYNCHUS KISUTCH)

The Coho Salmon, also known as the Silver Salmon, is one of seven species of Pacific salmon. It is found from Alaska to central California, although the central California population is estimated at only 1 to 5 percent of its historical levels. It grows to 24 to 30 inches in length and weighs from 8 to 12 pounds.

Red-bellied Piranha

(PYGOCENTRUS NATTEREN)

The Red-bellied Piranha is found only in the Amazon River basin in South America. It has razor-sharp teeth and a relentless bite. In 1913, Theodore Roosevelt described it as "the most ferocious fish in the world." It normally lives about 10 years.

Stoplight Parrotfish

(SPARISOMA VIRIDE)

The Stoplight Parrotfish is one of 90 species of parrotfish, which get their name from the shape of their teeth, which grow into a parrot-like beak. It is found in the Caribbean, Florida, and the Gulf of Mexico. It is a protogynous hermaphrodite, which means that it is born female and transitions to male. It is herbivorous and adults are from 12 to 20 inches in length.

Stonefish

(SYNANCEIA VERRUCOSA)

The Stonefish is the most venomous fish in the world. It protects itself by injecting a venom through its dorsal fin spines which can kill an adult human in under an hour. It hides on the sea floor, where it waits patiently, camouflaged, for its prey to come near, before snapping it up. Its diet is usually reef fishes and invertebrates. It lives in the Indo-Pacific region.

Yellow Tang
(ZEBRASOMA FLAVESCENS)

The Yellow Tang is a small surgeonfish, measuring up to 8 inches in length. It is mostly found in the subtropical waters from Hawaii to Japan, although it can also be found in most saltwater environments. It is popular with those who maintain saltwater aquariums. It can live up to 30 years in the wild, but only 5 to 10 years in captivity.

Clownfish
(AMPHIPRION OCELLARIS)

Clownfish are found in the warm waters of sheltered reefs in the Red Sea and Pacific Ocean. They reach an average of only 3 inches in length. They live in groups of males, with one dominant female in charge. If the dominant female dies, the dominant male transitions to a female and takes charge of the group.

Ringtail Surgeonfish

(ACANTHURUS BLOCHII)

The Ringtail Surgeonfish, also known as the Tailring Surgeonfish, is found in lagoons and seaweed reefs from the eastern coast of Africa to Hawaii and from Japan to Australia. It originated in Indonesia and achieves a maximum length of 17 inches. It feeds on algae and seaweed.

Yellowtail Damselfish
(CHRYSIPTERA PARASEMA)

The Yellowtail Damselfish is a popular saltwater aquarium fish that is found in the reefs of the Indian and Pacific Oceans. Its maximum size is about 3 inches, with a weight of 10 ounces. It is aggressive towards other aquarium fish. It lives from 2 to 6 years in the wild, but in ideal environmental conditions it may live up to 15 years.

Asian Sheepshead Wrasse

(SEMICOSSYPHUS RETICULATUS)

The Asian Sheepshead Wrasse is one of the largest species of wrasse. It is native to the western Pacific Ocean. It inhabits rocky reef areas in the Korean Peninsula, China, and Japan.

Moorish Idol Fish

(ZANCLUS CORNUTUS)

The Moorish Idol Fish is a small (7 to 9 inches in length) inhabitant of coral reefs and lagoons in the Pacific and Indian Oceans. It eats algae and small invertebrates. It lives for two to four years in the wild, but only one year in captivity.

Bargibant's Pygmy Seahorse
(HIPPOCAMPUS BARGIBANTI)

Bargibant's Pygmy Seahorse is the smallest seahorse species that has been discovered and is named after Georges Bargibant, who found it in 1969. It lives from Japan to Australia, although with its small size (.79 inches in length) and camouflage coloration, it is very difficult to obtain much information about it.

Yellowfin Tuna
(THUNNUS ALBACARES)

The Yellowfin Tuna is highly migratory and can be found in the Atlantic, Pacific, and Indian Oceans. About the only place it is not found is the Mediterranean Sea. It has an average lifespan of 6 to 7 years. It is very popular among fishermen, as its average size is 450 pounds and 100 inches in length. The largest recorded weighed 880 pounds.

Spotted Ratfish

(HYDROLAGUS COLLIEI)

The Spotted Ratfish is closely related to sharks and rays. It is found in the northeastern Pacific Ocean and lives near the sea floor amid the mud and rocky bottoms. Its prey, which includes clams, crabs, and shrimp, it finds by its sense of smell. It averages about 23 inches in length.

Elephant Fish

(CALLORHINCHUS MILII)

The Elephant Fish, also known as the Australian Ghostshark, is found in southern Australia, Tasmania, and New Zealand. It uses its hoe-shaped snout to probe the ocean bottom for invertebrates and small fish. It grows to a maximum length of about 4.9 feet.

Bluefin Trevally

(CARANX MELAMPYGUS)

The Bluefin Trevally inhabits the Indo-Pacific region and the eastern Pacific from Mexico to Panama. It is an ambush predator, attacking sardines, anchovies, small mackerel, crabs, shrimp, and squid from hiding places. The largest known Bluefin Trevally was 3.8 feet long.

Leaf Scorpionfish

(TAENIANOTUS TRIACANTHUS)

The Leaf Scorpionfish, also known as the Paper Fish, is found off the east coast of Africa all the way to Ecuador and from Japan and Hawaii to Australia. The largest ever found was only 3.9 inches long. It spends most of its time hiding motionless among algae and sea grass -- imitating a leaf swaying in the water.

Ocean Sunfish
(MOLA MOLA)

The Ocean Sunfish, or Common Mola, is the heaviest known bonefish in the world. Adults average 10 feet in length and weigh an average of 2,000 pounds. It is found in tropical and temperate waters worldwide and its favorite food is the jellyfish. It likes to sunbathe close to the ocean surface but can dive to depths of 2,600 feet.

Sockeye Salmon

(ONCORHYNCHUS NERKA)

The Sockeye Salmon, also known as the Red Salmon, is one of the smaller Pacific salmon species at 18 to 31 inches in length and a weight of 4 to 15 pounds, but it is the most important species of salmon to the economy of Alaska. Its lifespan is from three to seven years.

Bumphead Parrotfish

(BOLBOMETOPAN MURICATUM)

The Bumphead Parrotfish, also known as the Humphead Parrotfish or the Green Humphead Parrotfish, is the largest species of parrotfish, growing to a length of 4.2 feet and weighing up to 100 pounds. It is found in many oceanic coral reefs and can live to 40 years of age.

Titan Triggerfish

(BALISTOIDES VIRIDESCENS)

The Titan Triggerfish, also known as the Moustache Triggerfish, is the largest of the species, weighing up to 30 pounds and stretching up to 30 inches in length. It is very aggressive and dangerous, with powerful teeth that can seriously harm divers. It is found in the Indo-Pacific region and will live about 8 years in the wild and 20 years in captivity.

World of Fish

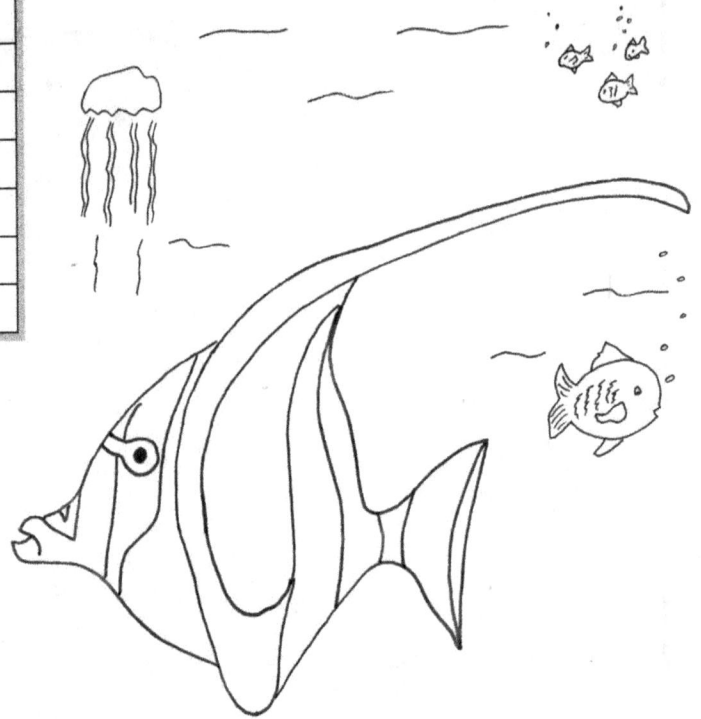

Across

2. _____ King; another name for Atlantic Tarpon.

3. _____ Fish; Also known as the Australian Ghostshark.

6. Red-bellied _____; It's only found in the Amazon River basin.

7. _____ Scorpionfish; Also known as the Paper Fish.

9. Spotted _____; Finds Its prey with its sense of smell.

10. _____ Salmon; Also known as the Silver Salmon.

12. _____ Dolphinfish; Another name for Mahi Mahi.

14. The Powder Blue Surgeonfish in "Finding Nemo."

Down

1. _____ Unicornfish; Also known as the Blonde Naso Tang.

2. The world's most venomous fish.

4. Bluehead _____; It changes color to match its surroundings.

5. Planehead _____; It is found from Morocco to Angola.

8. _____ Triggerfish; Also known as the Moustache Triggerfish.

11. _____ Salmon; Also known as the Red Salmon.

13. _____ Sunfish; Also known as the Common Mola.

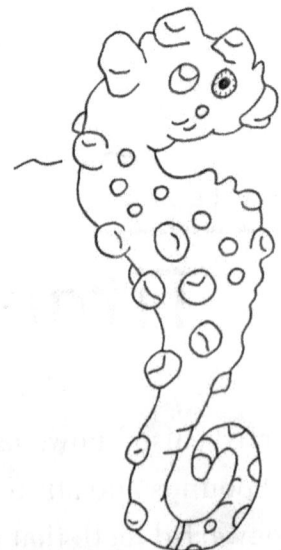

Jerry Cavanaugh

Jerry Cavanaugh is a former high school and middle school teacher, whose areas of expertise include history, psychology, and English. He was born and raised in Iowa, taught 35 years in the Davenport, Iowa, public schools, and now lives in Florida.

Also By Jerry Cavanaugh

From Newhouse Creative Group

Dr. C's Cool Clues and Cartoons: The Presidents
Dr. C's Cool Clues and Cartoons: African Americans

Superwomen: 60 American Heroines
Presidential Tweets from Washington to Trump
Illustrivia: Illustrated Trivia Items (series of nine books)
Awesome to Absurd: Quotations to Guide Your Life...or Not
From Cairo to Kazakhstan: A Journal of Teaching Overseas
Two Years in Thailand: A Journal of Teaching Overseas
That's Why I'm Here: A Memoir
Caricatures by Cavanaugh: Senior Softball in the Villages

Inspiring the readers and writers of today and tomorrow!

Visit AimHiPress.com for more books and other products from AimHi Press
and the rest of the Newhouse Creative Group family!

Newhouse Creative Group

Inspiring the readers and writers of today and tomorrow!

FREE Book for Subscribing to The NCG Narrative

Subscribe to our free newsletter, The NCG Narrative, to immediately receive a **FREE** eBook from Newhouse Creative Group.

Be the first to learn about NCG's newest releases, get behind the scenes of NCG, enter NCG Narrative exclusive contests and giveaways, and much more!

Subscribe today at NewhouseCreativeGroup.com

www.ingramcontent.com/pod-product-compliance
Lightning Source LLC
Chambersburg PA
CBHW051347290326
41933CB00042B/3324